COLOR STRUCK

A PLAY

By

ZORA NEALE HURSTON

INCLUDING THE
INTRODUCTORY ESSAY
*A Brief History of
the Harlem Renaissance*

First published in 1926

Read & Co.

Copyright © 2022 Read & Co. Books

This edition is published by Read & Co. Books,
an imprint of Read & Co.

This book is copyright and may not be reproduced or copied in any
way without the express permission of the publisher in writing.

British Library Cataloguing-in-Publication Data
A catalogue record for this book is available
from the British Library.

Read & Co. is part of Read Books Ltd.
For more information visit
www.readandcobooks.co.uk

CONTENTS

A BRIEF
HISTORY OF THE
HARLEM RENAISSANCE

The period of the Harlem Renaissance between the 1910s and the 1930s was a hotbed of African American artistic and cultural revival. Coined as "the New Negro Movement" by Alain Locke, it took place in the three square miles of Harlem, New York, in what became the centre of African American artistic opportunity. It was a time and a place that was prominent for Black creatives, becoming an influential microcosm of talent across the fields of art, literature, music, and more. The likes of Langston Hughes and Zora Neal Hurston, along with their contemporaries like James Weldon Johnson, Countee Cullen, Alice Dunbar Nelson, W.E.B. Du Bois, Nella Larson, Claude McKay, Jean Toomer, Anne Spencer and Angelina Weld Grimké were all prominent writers, artists and thinkers during the time. Each created work that would go on to establish a new African American identity within the late-modern era, from poetry to essays to novels, all rooted in the unique Black experience. Labelled "the Negro capital of the world" by one of its most prominent literary figures, James Weldon Johnson, the neighbourhood of Harlem was a catalyst for creative talent.

As a consequence of the Great Migration of African Americans from the southern states, Harlem became an area of prolific social and cultural change. The mass internal movement saw people travel north seeking higher-paid work and education opportunities and, most prominently, freedom from Jim Crow laws' oppression. The First World War had displaced many of the low-wage European labourers back to their homes, allowing jobs in the bigger cities to be filled by African Americans escaping the racial segregation and prolific lynchings in the American South. While a cultural revolution was also happening across the country in northern cities like Philadelphia and Chicago, the neighbourhood of Harlem in New York was its epicentre. The mounting industrialisation and opportunities brought about by the War drew rural people to the cities, searching for work. This resulted in growing communities of African Americans in places like Harlem, creating an environment that encouraged a new culture to thrive. A flux of Black-owned businesses brought more people to the neighbourhood making for a flourishing community of African Americans in the heart of New York City, eager to carve a new future as free people.

Many of the leading African American writers of the era lived and worked within Harlem during the 1920s. James Weldon Johnson was an American poet, writer, and civil rights activist who moved to the area after serving in the War, arriving at the zenith of the Harlem Renaissance. His work celebrated the power of Black culture. It was steeped in the realities of the African American experience, using a Black vernacular throughout his later works to tackle some of the broader socio-political issues surrounding racial prejudice. His poetic contemporary Claude McKay was another central figure in the movement, shrouding his work's political angle under poetic gauze. His most famous poem, "If We Must Die", published in 1919, became a prominent statement against the wave of Black discrimination and lynchings that followed the end of the First World War. The poem spurred a new wave of political awareness, and is often seen as a precursor for the liberal work that would follow. His seminal 1922 poetry collection *Harlem Shadows* spotlighted the difficult lives of African Americans and showcased the revolutionary spirit of the time.

Encouraged by prolific writer and philosopher Alain Locke, a new wave of young artists utilised the changing societal landscape in the 1920s. They created uncompromising works in their depictions of Black life in an attempt to reclaim an authentic African American identity, one that rejected the degrading and often racist stereotypes attached to their culture. As a new awareness around African American identity was formed, civil rights groups like the National Association for the Advancement of Coloured People (NAACP) were established, issuing journals that celebrated young writers tackling social and political problems. Journals like *The Crisis* and *Fire!!* became beacons of African American creativity and voice, enabling white publishing houses and readers more access to the rich diversity of Black arts.

By the mid-1920s, the American Jazz Age was in full swing. The music produced in Harlem by the likes of Louis Armstrong and Duke Ellington filled the clubs in the city, gaining fashionable status amongst white audiences. Iconic places like the Cotton Club and Small's Paradise were established to provide Black entertainment to white customers. Originating in New Orleans, Louisiana, through the enslaved African American communities, the jazz genre was a statement of freedom. It stood for freedom from oppression and white cultural sensibilities, eventually becoming the soundtrack to the hedonistic era, infusing all aspects of society from literature to fashion. Prolific poet Langston Hughes filled his work with the jazz music of his culture, infusing it with the rhythms of ragtime and blues to create a new literary art form - Jazz Poetry. Best known as the figurehead of the Harlem Renaissance, his work inspired that of James Weldon Johnson, whose poems were rich with the same musical rhythm.

The focus on the urban Black experience had shifted exterior perceptions of African Americans from lowly rural folk to one of cosmopolitan sophistication, which consequentially spurred a movement for political change and artistic freedom within their culture. This ever-developing form of a new Black identity created room for queer culture to appear. Unconventional lifestyles were welcomed in Harlem, with queer culture thriving in the blues scene. While it was still illegal to engage in homosexual acts, much of the culture lived underground in clubs and bars. Prominent figures of the time like Gertrude 'Ma' Rainey (later dubbed 'Mother of Blues') and author Zora Neal Hurston were romantically linked to other women. Rainey and her contemporary Gladys Bentley were known to cross-dress, hosting drag nights amongst the safe havens of Harlem. The movement actively challenged gender roles and race issues, embracing feminism and queer culture, placing it far ahead of America at the time.

The playwright and poet Angelina Weld Grimké paved the way for such freedoms with her early play *Rachel*. Considered the first show of the movement in 1916, Grimké created a work that attacked the patriarchy at its core. An entirely Black troop performed the three-act-drama, purposefully created for the civil rights group the NAACP. It was a rebuttal against the recently released film *The Birth of Nation* (1915), which glorified the Ku Klux Klan and portrayed a horrifically racist view of Black people and their role in the American Civil War. The play narrates the life of an African American family in the northern states after the Great Migration and disregards the common degrading caricatures found in theatre at the time. The titular character challenges the Black stereotype by exploring different reactions to the widespread racial discrimination felt at the time. Grimké subtly articulated her lesbianism within her works, with some of her later unpublished poems expressing the sexual suppression she felt throughout her life. *Rachel*, created by a queer Black female author, has come to represent the beginning of the movement, a forerunner for the ground breaking work that would go on to establish this era as one of the significant political and creative periods in African American history.

Following in her wake was Zora Neale Hurston. She became one of the most eminent female authors of the time, penning over fifty works, including novels, short stories, plays and essays, all portraying the racial struggles of African Americans in the early

1900s. Tackling contemporary issues in the Black community, her works were published in the prolific African American journal *Fire!!* established by herself, along with writers such as Wallace Henry Thurman, Countee Cullen, Langston Hughes and artists Aaron Douglass and Richard Bruce Nugent. Together, they explored many controversial issues within the Black community through the voices of younger authors, touching on topics such as homosexuality, promiscuity, prostitution and colour prejudice.

This prosperous time in Harlem ended abruptly with the Wall Street Crash of 1929, promptly followed by the Great Depression. While artists and writers continued to create work, the wave of opportunity was ceasing. However, their work was not in vain. The outstanding contribution to all creative fields laid the foundation for the Black Arts Movement of the 1960s. It brought around new awareness for Black art, one that was considered serious in the elite art world. Artists and writers continued dealing with issues like race and sexuality while exploring the everchanging African American experience. The new Black identity forged in the centre of the movement also caused a rippling effect regarding political justice. A product of the ongoing persecution of Black people across the country and the continued racial segregation laws, the newfound sense of African American independence felt in this period forced a new awareness of civil and political rights, consequently leading to race riots and the monumental Civil Rights Act of 1964.

While this was a pivotal time for African American culture, it was not without its critics. The major cultural reawakening that secured a new and unique identity within the wider American society was brandished by some as an assimilation of dominant white culture rather than an authentically African-American one. Although the socio-political landscape of the time determined the boundaries in which Black people could create a life for themselves, they were criticised for utilising what small freedoms they had to find their voice. Even from the artist's perspective, debates were held about how far they could push the boundaries to avoid playing further into the general and often negative stereotype. Harlem Renaissance author W.E.B Du Bois coined the term "double consciousness" in his work, *The Souls of Black Folk* (1903), to represent the duality in identity that formed at the meeting point between Black and American culture. It articulated a way to understand the expression of the newly forged identity of African-American people, with a heightened awareness of its reception by those outside of it.

As labelled by Alain Locke, this "spiritual coming of age" saw African American artists and thinkers seize the moment of group expression and carve out a new identity for themselves at the beginning of the twentieth century. While the movement was not confined to Harlem, the district became well-known as the centre of Black creative talent. A prolific time in American cultural history, the prominent creatives of the Harlem Renaissance created a new world for the generations to follow, establishing a new Black identity and awareness of such in wider society through their often poignant and thought-provoking work.

COLOR STRUCK

PERSONS

JOHN — A light brown-skinned man
EMMALINE — A black woman
WESLEY — A boy who plays an accordion
EMMALINE'S DAUGHTER — A very white girl
EFFIE — A mulatto girl
A RAILWAY CONDUCTOR
A DOCTOR
Several who play mouth organs, guitars, banjos.
Dancers, passengers, etc

SCENE I

TIME.—*Twenty years ago and present.*
PLACE.—*A Southern City.*

SETTING.—*Early night. The inside of a "Jim Crow" railway coach. The car is parallel to the footlights. The seats on the down stage side of the coach are omitted. There are the luggage racks above the seats. The windows are all open. They are exits in each end of the car—right and left.*

ACTION.—*Before the curtain goes up there is the sound of a locomotive whistle and a stopping engine, loud laughter, many people speaking at once, good-natured shreiks, strumming of stringed instruments, etc. The ascending curtain discovers a happy lot of Negroes boarding the train dressed in the gaudy, twdry best of 1900. They are mostly in couples—each couple bearing a covered-over market basket which the men hastily deposit in the racks as they scramble for seats. There is a litle friendly pushing and shoving. One pair just miss a seat three times, much to the enjoyment of the crowd. Many "plug" silk hats are in evidence, also sun-flowers in button holes. The women are showily dressed in the manner of the time, and quite conscious of their finery. A few seats remain unoccupied.*

Enter Effie (left) above, with a basket.

ONE OF THE MEN (*standing, lifting his "plug" in a grand manner*). Howdy do, Miss Effie, you'se lookin' jes lak a rose.

*(Effie blushes and is confused.
She looks up and down for a seat.)*

Fack is, if you wuzn't walkin' long, ah'd think you wuz a rose— *(he looks timidly behind her and the others laugh).* Looka here, where's Sam at?

EFFIE *(tossing her head haughtily).* I don't know an' I don't keer.

THE MAN *(visibly relieved).* Then lemme scorch you to a seat. *(He takes her basket and leads her to a seat center of the car, puts the basket in the rack and seats himself beside her with his hat at a rakish angle.)*

MAN *(sliding his arm along the back of the seat).* How come Sam ain't heah—y'll on a bust?

EFFIE *(angrily).* A man dat don't buy me nothin tuh put in *mah* basket, ain't goin' wid *me* tuh no cake walk. *(The hand on the seat touches her shoulder and she thrusts it away).* Take yo' arms from 'round me, Dinky! Gwan hug yo' Ada!

MAN *(in mock indignation).* Do you think I'd look at Ada when Ah got a chance tuh be wid you? Ah always wuz sweet on you, but you let ole Mullet-head Sam cut me out.

ANOTHER MAN *(with head out of the window).* Just look at de darkies coming! *(With head insite coach.)* Hey, Dinky! Heah come Ada wid a great big basket.

(Dinky jumps up from beside Effie and rushes to exit right. In a moment they're-enter and take a seat near entrance. Everyone in coach laughs. Dinky's girl turns and calls back to Effie.)

GIRL. Where's Sam, Effie?

EFFIE. Lawd knows, Ada.

GIRL. Lawd a mussy! Who you gointer walk de cake wid?

EFFIE. Nobody, Ah reckon. John and Emma gointer win it nohow. They's the bestest cake-walkers in dis state.

ADA. You'se better than Emma any day in de week. Cose Sam cain't walk lake John. *(She stands up and scans the coach.)* Looka heah, ain't John an' Emma going? They ain't on heah!

(The locomotive bell begins to ring.)

EFFIE. Mah Gawd, s'pose dey got left!

MAN *(with head out of window)*. Heah they come, nip and tuck— whoo-ee! They'se gonna make it! *(He waves excitedly.)* Come on Jawn! *(Everybody crowds the windows, encouraging them by gesture and calls. As the whistle blows twice, and the train begins to move, they enter panting and laughing at left. The only seat left is the one directly in front of Effie.)*

DINKY *(standing)*. Don't y'all skeer us no mo' lake dat! There couldn't be no cake walk thout y'all. Dem shad-mouf St. Augustine coons would win dat cake and we would have tuh kill 'em all bodaciously.

JOHN. It was Emmaline nearly made us get left. She says I wuz smiling at Effie on the street car and she had to get off and wait for another one.

EMMA *(removing the hatpins from her hat, turns furiously upon him)*. You wuz grinning at her and she wuz grinning back jes lake a ole chessy cat!

JOHN. *(positively)*. I wuzn't.

EMMA *(about to place her hat in rack)*. You wuz. I seen you looking jes lake a possum.

JOHN. I wuzn't. I never gits a chance tuh smile at nobody—you won't let me.

EMMA. Jes the same every time you sees a yaller face, you takes a chance. *(They sit down in peeved silence for a minute.)*

DINKY. Ada, les we all sample de basket. I bet you got huckleberry pie.

ADA. No I aint, I got peach an' tater pies, but we aint gonna tetch
a thing tell we gits tuh de hall.
DINKY (*mock alarm*). Naw, don't do dat! It's all right tuh save the
fried chicken, but pies is *always* et on trains.
ADA. Aw shet up! (*He struggles with her for a kiss. She slaps him
but finally yields.*)
JOHN (*looking behind him*). Hellow, Effie, where's Sam?
EFFIE. Deed, I don't know.
JOHN. Y'all on a bust?
EMMA. None ah yo' bizness, you got enough tuh mind yo' own
self. Turn 'round!

> (*She puts up a pouting mouth and he snatches a kiss.
> She laughs just as he kisses her again and there is a
> resounding smack which causes the crowd to laugh.
> And cries of* "Oh you kid!" "Salty dog!")

> (*Enter conductor left calling tickets cheerfully and laughing at
> the general merriment.*)

CONDUCTOR. I hope somebody from Jacksonville wins this cake.
JOHN. You live in the "Big Jack?"
CONDUCTOR. Sure do. And I wanta taste a piece of that cake on
the way back tonight.
JOHN. Jes rest easy—them Augustiners aint gonna smell it.
(*Turns to Emma.*) Is they, baby?
EMMA. Not if Ah kin help it.

> (*Somebody with a guitar sings*:
> "Ho babe, mah honey taint no lie.")

> (*The conductor takes up tickets, passes on and exits right.*)

WESLEY. Look heah, you cake walkers—y'all oughter git up and limber up yo' joints. I heard them folks over to St. Augustine been oiling up wid goose-grease, and over to Ocala they been rubbing down in snake oil.

A WOMAN'S VOICE. You better shut up, Wesley, you just joined de church last month. Somebody's going to tell the pastor on you.

WESLEY. Tell it, tell it, take it up and smell it. Come on out you John and Emma and Effie, and limber up.

JOHN. Naw, we don't wanta do our walking steps—nobody won't wanta see them when we step out at the hall. But we kin do something else just to warm ourselves up.

(Wesley begins to play "Goo Goo Eyes" on his accordian, the other instruments come in one by one and John and Emma step into the aisle and "parade" up and down the aisle—Emma holding up her skirt, showing the lace on her petticoats. They two-step back to their seat amid much applause.)

WESLEY. Come on out, Effie! Sam aint heah so you got to hold up his side too. Step on out.

(There is a murmur of applause as she steps into the aisle. Wesley strikes up "I'm gointer live anyhow till I die" It is played quite spiritedly as Effie swings into the pas-me-la—)

WESLEY *(in ecstasy)*. Hot stuff I reckon! Hot stuff I reckon!

(The musicians are stamping. Great enthusiasm. Some clap time with hands and feet. She hurls herself into a modified Hoochy Koochy, and finishes up with an ecstatic yell.)

(There is a babble of talk and laughter and exultation.)

JOHN (*applauding loudly*). If dat Effie can't step nobody can.

EMMA. Course you'd say so cause it's her. Everything she do is pretty to you.

JOHN (*caressing her*). Now don't say that, Honey. Dancing is dancing no matter who is doing it. But nobody can hold a candle to you in nothing.

(*Some men are heard tuning up—getting pitch to sing. Four of them crowd together in one seat and begin the chorus of "Daisies Won't Tell" John and Emma grow quite affectionate.*)

JOHN (*kisses her*). Emma, what makes you always picking a fuss with me over some yaller girl.
What makes you so jealous, nohow? I don't do nothing.

(*She clings to him, but he turns slightly away. The train whistle blows, there is a slackening of speed. Passengers begin to take down baskets from their racks.*)

EMMA. John! John, don't you want me to love you, honey?

JOHN (*turns and kisses her slowly*). Yes, I want you to love me, you know I do. But I don't like to be accused o' ever light colored girl in the world. It hurts my feeling. I don't want to be jealous like you are.

(*Enter at right Conductor, crying "St. Augustine, St. Augustine." He exits left. The crowd has congregated at the two exits, pushing good-naturedly and joking. All except John and Emma. They are still seated with their arms about each other.*)

EMMA (*sadly*). Then you don't want my love, John, cause I can't help mahself from being jealous. I loves you so hard, John, and jealous love is the only kind I got.

(*John kisses her very feelingly.*)

EMMA. Just for myself alone is the only way I knows how to love.

(They are standing in the aisle with their arms about each other as the curtain falls.)

SCENE II

SETTING—A weather-board hall. A large room with the joists bare. The place has been divided by a curtain of sheets stretched and a rope across from left to right. From behind the curtain there are occasional sounds of laughter, a note or two on a stringed instrument or accordion. General stir. That is the dance hall. The front is the ante-room where the refreshments are being served. A "plank" seat runs all around the hall, along the walls. The lights are kerosene lamps with reflectors. They are fixed to the wall. The lunch-baskets are under the seat. There is a table on either side upstage with a woman behind each. At one, ice cream is sold, at the other, roasted peanuts and large red-and-white sticks of peppermint candy.

People come in by twos and three, laughing, joking, horse-plays, gauchily flowered dresses, small waists, bulging hips and busts, hats worn far back on the head, etc. People from Ocala greet others from Palatka, Jacksonville, St. Augustine, etc.

Some find seats in the ante-room, others pass on into the main hall. Enter the Jacksonville delegation, laughing, pushing proudly.

DINKY. Here we is, folks—here we *is*. Gointer take dat cake on back tuh Jacksonville where it belongs.
MAN. Gwan! Whut wid you mullet-head Jacksonville Coons know whut to do wid a cake. It's gointer stay right here in Augustine where de good cake walkers grow.

DINKY. Taint no 'Walkers' never walked till John and Emmaline prance out—you mighty come a tootin'.

(*Great langhing and joshing as more people come in. John and Emma are encouraged, urged on to win.*)

EMMA. Let's we git a seat, John, and set down.
JOHN. Sho will—nice one right over there. (*They push over to wall seat, place basket underneath, and sit. Newcomers shake hands with them and urge them on to win.*)

(*Enter Joe Clarke and a small group. He is a rotund, expansive man with a liberal watch chain and charm.*)

DINKY (*slapping Clarke on the back*). If you don't go 'way from here! Lawdy, if it aint Joe.
CLARKE (*jovially*). Ah thought you had done forgot us people in Eatonville since you been living up here in Jacksonville.
DINKY. Course Ah aint. (*Turning.*) Looka heah folks! Joe Clarke oughta be made chairman uh dis meetin'—Ah mean Past Great-Grand Master of Ceremonies, him being the onliest mayor of de onliest colored town in de state.
GENERAL CHORUS. Yeah, let him be—thass fine, etc.
DINKY (*setting his hat at a new angle and throwing out his chest*). And *Ah'll* scorch him to de platform. Ahem!

(*Sprinkling of laughter as Joe Clarke is escorted into next room by Dinky.*)

(*The musicians are arriving one by one during this time. A guitar, accordian, mouth organ, banjo, etc. Soon there is a rapping for order heard inside and the voice of Joe Clarke.*)

JOE CLARKE. Git yo' partners one an' all for de gran' march! Git yo' partners, gent-mens!
A MAN (*drawing basket from under bench*). Let's we all eat first.

(John and Emma go buy ice-cream. They coquettishly eat from each other's spoons. Old Man Lizzimore crosses to Effie and removes his hat and bows with a great flourish.)

LIZZIMORE. Sam ain't here t'night, is he, Effie.
EFFIE (*embarrassed*). Naw suh, he aint.
LIZZ. Well, you like chicken? (*Extends arm to her.*) Take a wing!

(He struts her up to the table amid the laughter of the house. He wears no collar.)

JOHN (*squeezes Emma's hand*). You certainly is a ever loving mamma—when you aint mad.
EMMA (*smiles sheepishly*). You oughtn't to make me mad then.
JOHN. Ah don't make you! You makes yo'self mad, den blame it on me. Ah keep on tellin' you Ah don't love nobody but you. Ah knows heaps uh half-white girls Ah could git ef Ah wanted to. But (*he squeezes her hard again*) Ah jus' wants you! You know what they say! De darker de berry, de sweeter de taste!
EMMA (*pretending to pout*). Oh, you tries to run over me an' keep it under de cover, but Ah won't let yuh. (*Both laugh.*) Les' we eat our basket!
JOHN. Alright. (*He pulls the basket out and she removes the table cloth. They set the basket on their knees and begin to eat fried chicken.*)
MALE VOICE. Les' everybody eat—motion's done carried.

(Everybody begins to open baskets. All have fried chicken. Very good humor prevails. Delicacies are swapped from one basket to the other. John and Emma offer the man next them some supper. He takes a chicken leg. Effie crosses to John and Emma with two pieces of pie on a plate.)

EFFIE. Y'll have a piece uh mah blueberry pie—it's mighty nice!

(*She proffers it with a timid smile to Emma
who "freezes" up instantly.*)

EMMA. Naw! We don't want no pie. We got cocoanut layer-cake.
JOHN. Ah—Ah think ah'd choose a piece uh pie, Effie. (*He takes
it.*) Will you set down an' have a snack wid us? (*He slides
over to make room.*)
EFFIE (*mervously*). Ah, naw, Ah got to run on back to mah basket,
but Ah thought maybe y'll mout' want tuh taste mah pie.

(*She turns to go.*)

JOHN. Thank you, Effie. It's mighty good, too.

(*He eats it. Effie crosses to her seat. Emma glares at her for
a minute, then turns disgustedly away from the basket. John
catches her shoulder and faces her around.*)

JOHN (*pleadingly*). Honey, be nice. Don't act lak dat!
EMMA (*jerking free*). Naw, you done ruint mah appetite now,
carryin' on wid dat punkin-colored ole gal.
JOHN. Whut kin Ah do? If you had a acted polite Ah wouldn't a
had nothin' to say.
EMMA. Naw, youse jus' hog-wile ovah her cause she's half-white!
No matter whut Ah say, you keep carryin' on wid her.
Act polite? Naw Ah aint gonna be deceitful an' bust mah
gizzard fuh nobody! Let her keep her dirty ole pie ovah
there where she is!
JOHN (*looking around to see if they are overheard*). Sh-sh! Honey,
you mustn't talk so loud.
EMMA (*louder*). Ah-Ah aint gonna bite mah tongue! If she don't
like it she can lump it. Mah back is broad—(*John tries
to cover her mouth with his hand*). She calls herself a big
cigar, but I kin smoke her!

*(The people are laughing and talking for the most part and pay
no attention. Effie is laughing and talking to those around her
and does not hear the tirade. The eating is over and everyone is
going behind the curtain. John and Emma put away their basket
like the others, and sit glum. Voice of Master-of-ceremonies can
be heard from beyond curtain announcing the pas-me-la contest.
The contestants, mostly girls, take the floor. There is no music
except the clapping of hands and the shouts of "Parse-me-lah"
in time with the hand-clapping. At the end Master announces
winner. Shadows seen on curtain.)*

MASTER. Mathilda Clarke is winner—if she will step forward she
will receive a beautiful wook fascinator. *(The girl goes up
and receives it with great hand-clapping and good humor.)*
And now since the roosters is crowin' foah midnight, an'
most of us got to git up an' go to work tomorrow, The Great
Cake Walk will begin. Ah wants de floor cleared, cause
de representatives of de several cities will be announced
an' we wants em to take de floor as their names is called.
Den we wants 'em to do a gran' promenade roun' de hall.
An' they will then commence to walk fuh de biggest
cake ever baked in dis state. Ten dozen eggs—ten
pounds of flour—ten pounds of butter, and so on and so
forth. Now then—*(he strikes a pose)* for St. Augustine—
Miss Lucy Taylor, Mr. Ned Coles.

(They step out amid applause and stand before stage.)

For Daytona—Miss Janie Bradley, Enoch Nixon

(Same business.)

For Ocala—Miss Docia Boger, Mr. Oscar Clarke

(Same business.)

For Palatka—Miss Maggie Lemmons, Mr. Senator Lewis

(*Same business*)

And for Jacksonville the most popular "walkers" in de state—Miss Emmaline Beazeby, Mr. John Turner.

(*Tremendous applause. John rises and offers his arm grandiloquently to Emma.*)

EMMA (*pleadingly, and clutching his coat*). John let's we all don't go in there with all them. Let's we all go on home.

JOHN (*amazed*). Why, Emma?

EMMA. Cause, cause all them girls is going to pulling and hauling on you, and—

JOHN (*impatiently*). Shucks! Come on. Don't you hear the people clapping for us and calling our names? Come on!

(*He tries to pull her up—she tries to drag him back.*)

Come on, Emma! Taint no sense in your acting like this. The band is playing for us. Hear 'em? (*He moves feet in a dance step.*)

EMMA. Naw, Jobn, Ah'm skeered. I loves you—I—

(*He tries to break away from her. She is holding on fiercely.*)

JOHN. I got to go! I been practising almost a year—I—we done come all the way down here. I can walk the cake, Emma—we got to—I got to go in! (*He looks into her face and sees her tremendous fear.*) What you skeered about?

EMMA (*hopefully*). You won't go it—You'll come on go home with me all by ourselves. Come on John. I can't, I just can't go in there and see all them girls—Effie hanging after you—.

JOHN. I got to go in—(*he removes her hand from his coat*)— whether you come with me or not.

EMMA. Oh—them yaller wenches! How I hate 'em! They gets everything they wants—.

VOICE INSIDE. We are waiting for the couple from Jacksonville— Jacksonville! Where is the couple from—.

(*Wesley parts the curtain and looks out.*)

WESLEY. Here they is out here spooning! You all can't even hear your names called. Come on John and Emma.

JOHN. Coming. (*He dashes inside. Wesley stands looking at Emma in surprise.*)

WESLEY. What's the matter, Emma? You and John spatting again? (*He goes back inside.*)

EMMA (*calmly bitter*). He went and left me. If we is spatting we done had our last one. (*She stands and clenches her fists.*) Ah, mah God! He's in there with her—Oh, them half whites, they gets everything, they gets everything everybody else wants! The men, the jobs—everything! The whole world is got a sign on it. Wanted: Light colored. Us blacks was made for cobble stones. (*She muffles a cry and sinks limp upon the seat.*)

VOICE INSIDE. Miss Effie Jones will walk for Jacksonville with Mr. John Turner in place of Miss Emmaline Beazeley.

SCENE III

DANCE HALL

*Emma springs to her feet and flings the curtains wide open.
She stands staring at the gay scene for a moment defiantly
then creeps over to a seat along the wall and shrinks into the
Spanish Moss, motionless.*

*Dance hall decorated with palmetto leaves and Spanish
Moss—a flag or two. Orchestra consists of guitar, mandolin,
banjo, accordian, church organ and drum.*

MASTER (*on platform*). Couples take yo' places! 'When de music
    starts, gentlemen parade yo' ladies once round de hall,
    den de walk begins. (*The music begins. Four men come
    out from behind the platform bearing a huge chocolate
    cake. The couples are "prancing" in their tracks. The men
    lead off the procession with the cake—the contestants
    make a grand slam around the hall.*)

MASTER. Couples to de floor! Stan' back, ladies an' gentlemen—
    give 'em plenty room.

*(Music changes to "Way Down in Georgia." Orchestra sings.
Effie takes the arm that John offers her and they parade to the
other end of the hall. She takes her place. John goes back upstage
to the platform, takes off his silk hat in a graceful sweep as he
bows deeply to Effie. She lifts her skirts and curtsies to the floor.
Both smile broadly. They advance toward each other, meet
midway, then, arm in arm, begin to "strut." John falters as he
faces her, but recovers promptly and is perfection in his style.)*

(Seven to nine minutes to curtain.) Fervor of spectators grows until all are taking part in some way—either hand-clapping or singing the words. At curtain they have reached frenzy.)

QUICK CURTAIN

(It stays down a few seconds to indicate ending of contest and goes up again on John and Effie being declared winners by Judges.)

MASTER *(on platform, with John and Effie on the floor before him).* By unanimous decision de cake goes to de couple from Jacksonville! *(Great enthusiasm. The cake is set down in the center of the floor and the winning couple parade around it arm in arm. John and Effie circle the cake happily and triumphantly. The other contestants, and then the entire assembly fall in behind and circle the cake, singing and clapping. The festivities continue. The Jacksonville quartet step upon the platform and sing a verse and chorus of "Daisies won't tell." Cries of "Hurrah for Jacksonville! Glory for the big town," "Hurrah for Big Jack.")*

A MAN *(seeing Emma).* You're from Jacksonville, aint you? *(He whirls her around and around.)* Aint you happy? Whoopee! *(He releases her and she drops upon a seat. She buries her face in the moss.)*

(Quartet begins on chorus again. People are departing, laughing, humming, with quartet cheering. John, the cake, and Effie being borne away in triumph.)

SCENE IV

TIME—*present. The interior of a one-room shack in an alley. There is a small window in the rear wall upstage left. There is an enlarged crayon drawing of a man and woman—man sitting cross-legged, a woman standing with her hand on his shoulder. A center table, red cover, a low, cheap rocker, two straight chairs, a small kitchen stove at left with a wood-box beside it, a water-bucket on a stand close by. A hand towel and a wash basin. A shelf of dishes above this. There is an ordinary oil lamp on the center table but it is not lighted when the curtain goes up. Some light enters through the window and falls on the woman seated in the low rocker. The door is center right. A cheap bed is against the upstage wall. Someone is on the bed but is lying so that the back is toward the audience.*

ACTION—*As the curtain rises, the woman is seen rocking to and fro in the low rocker. A dead silence except for the sound of the rocker and an occasional groan from the bed. Once a faint voice says "water" and the woman in the rocker arises and carries the tin dipper to the bed.*

WOMAN. No mo' right away—Doctor says not too much. (*Returns dipper to pail—Pause.*) You got right much fever—I better go git the doctor agin.

(*There comes a knocking at the door and she stands still for a moment, listening. It comes again and she goes to door but does not open it.*)

WOMAN. Who's that?

VOICE OUTSIDE. Does Emma Beasely live here?

EMMA. Yeah—(*pause*)—who is it?

VOICE. It's me—John Turner.

EMMA (*puts hands eagerly on the fastening*). John? did you say John Turner?

VOICE. Yes, Emma, it's me.

(*The door is opened and the man steps inside.*)

EMMA. John! Your hand (*she feels for it and touches it*). John flesh and blood.

JOHN (*laughing awkwardly*). It's me alright, old girl. Just as bright as a basket of chips. Make a light quick so I can see how you look. I'm crazy to see you. Twenty years is a long time to wait, Emma.

EMMA (*nervously*). Oh, let's we all just sit in the dark awhile. (*Apologetically.*) I wasn't expecting nobody and my house aint picked up. Sit down. (*She draws up the chair. She sits in rocker.*)

JOHN. Just to think! Emma! Me and Emma sitting down side by each. Know how I found you?

EMMA (*dully*). Naw. How?

JOHN (*brightly*). Soons I got in town I hunted up Wesley and he told me how to find you. That's who I come to see, you!

EMMA. Where you been all these years, up North somewheres? Nobody round here could find out where you got to.

JOHN. Yes, up North. Philadelphia.

EMMA. Married yet?

JOHN. Oh yes, seventeen years ago. But my wife is dead now and so I came as soon as it was decent to find you. I wants to marry you. I couldn't die happy if I didn't. Couldn't get over you—couldn't forget. Forget me, Emma?

EMMA. Naw, John. How could I?

JOHN (*leans over impulsively to catch her hand*). Oh, Emma, I love you so much. Strike a light honey so I can see you—see if you changed much. You was such a handsome girl!

EMMA. We don't exactly need no light, do we, John, tuh jus' set an' talk?

JOHN. Yes, we do, Honey. Ah wanna see you. Gwan, make a light.

(*There is a silence.*)

EMMA. Bet you' wife wuz some high-yaller dickty-doo.

JOHN. Naw she wasn't neither. She was jus' as much like you as Ah could get her. Make a light an' Ah'll show you her pictcher. Shucks, ah gotta look at mah old sweetheart. (*He strikes a match and holds it up between their faces and they look intently at each other over it until it burns out.*) You aint changed none atall, Emma, jus' as pretty as a speckled pup yet.

EMMA (*lighter*). Go long, John! (*Short pause*) 'member how you useter bring me magnolias?

JOHN. Do I? Gee, you was sweet! 'Member how Ah useter pull mah necktie loose so you could tie it back for me? Emma, Ah can't see to mah soul how we lived all this time, way from one another. 'Member how you useter make out mah ears had done run down and you useter screw 'em up agin for me?

(*They laugh.*)

EMMA. Yeah, Ah useter think you wuz gointer be mah husban' then—but you let dat ole—.

JOHN. Ah aint gonna let you alibi on me lak dat. Light dat lamp! You cain't lock me in de eye and say no such. (*He strikes another match and lights the lamp.*) Course, Ah don't wanta look too bossy, but Ah b'lieve you got to marry me tuh git rid of me. That is, if you aint married.

EMMA. Naw, Ah aint.

(*She turns the lamp down.*)

JOHN (*looking about the room*). Not so good, Emma. But wait till you see dat little place in Philly! Got a little "Rolls-Rough," too—gointer teach you to drive it, too.

EMMA. Ah been havin' a hard time, John, an' Ah lost you—oh, aint nothin' been right for me! Ah aint never been happy.

(*John takes both of her hands in his.*)

JOHN. You gointer be happy now, Emma. Cause Ah'm gointer make you. Gee Whiz! Ah aint but forty-two and you aint forty yet—we got plenty time. (There is a groan from the bed.) Gee, what's that?

EMMA (*ill at ease*). Thass mah chile. She's sick. Reckon Ah bettah see 'bout her.

JOHN. You got a chile? Gee, that great! Ah always wanted one. but didn't have no luck. Now we kin start off with a family. Girl or boy?

EMMA (*slowly*). A girl. Comin' tuh see me agin soon, John?

JOHN. Comin' agin? Ah aint gone yet! We aint talked, you aint kissed me an' nothin', and you aint showed me our girl. (*Another groan, more prolonged.*) She must be pretty sick—let's see. (*He turns in his chair and Emma rushes over to the bed and covers the girl securely, tucking her long hair under the covers, too—before he arises. He goes over to the bed and looks down into her face. She is mulatto. Turns to Emma teasingly.*) Talkin' 'bout me liking high-yallers—yo husband musta been pretty near white.

EMMA (*slowly*). Ah, never wuz married, John.

JOHN. It's alright, Emma. (*Kisses her warmly.*) Everything is going to be O.K. (*Turning back to the bed.*) Our child looks pretty sick, but she's pretty. (*Feels her forehead and cheek.*) Think she oughter have a doctor.

EMMA. Ah done had one. Course Ah cain't git no specialist an' nothin' lak dat. (*She looks about the room and his gaze follows hers.*) Ah aint got a whole lot lake you., Nobody don't git rich in no white-folks' kitchen, nor in de washtub. You know Ah aint no school-teacher an' nothin' lak dat.

(*John puts his arm about her.*)

JOHN. It's all right, Emma. But our daughter is bad off—run out an' git a doctor—she needs one. Ah'd go if Ah knowed where to find one—you kin git one the quickest—hurry, Emma.

EMMA (*looks from John to her daughter and back again.*) She'll be all right, Ah reckon, for a while. John, you love me—you really want me sho' nuff?

JOHN. Sure Ah do—think Ah'd come all de way down here for nothin'? Ah wants to marry agin.

EMMA. Soon, John?

JOHN. Real soon.

EMMA. Ah wuz jus' thinkin', mah folks is away now on a little trip—be home day after tomorrow —we could git married tomorrow.

JOHN. Al right. Now run on after the doctor —we must look after our girl. Gee, she's got a full suit of hair! Glad you didn't let her chop it off. (*Looks away from bed and sees Emma standing still.*)

JOHN. Emma, run on after the doctor, honey. (*She goes to the bed and again tucks the long braids of hair in, which are again pouring over the side of the bed by the feverish tossing of the girl.*) What's our daughter's name?

EMMA. Lou Lillian, (*She returns to the rocker uneasily and sits rocking jerkily. He returns to his seat and turns up the light.*)

JOHN. Gee, we're going to be happy—we gointer make up for all them twenty years (*another groan*). Emma, git up an' gwan git dat doctor. You done forgot Ah'm de boss uh dis family now—gwan, while Ah'm here to watch her whilst you're gone. Ah got to git back to mah stoppin'-place after a while.

EMMA. You go git one, John.

JOHN. Whilst Ah'm blunderin' round tryin' to find one, she'll be gettin' worse. She sounds pretty bad—(*takes out his wallet and hands her a bill*)—get a taxi if necessary. Hurry!

EMMA (*does not take the money, but tucks her arms and hair in again, and gives the girl a drink*). Reckon Ah better go git a doctor. Don't want nothin' to happen to *her*. After you left, Ah useter have such a hurtin' in heah (*touches bosom*) till she come an' eased it some.

JOHN. Here, take some money and get a good doctor. There must be some good colored ones around here now.

EMMA (*scornfully*). I wouldn't let one of 'em tend my cat if I had one! But let's we don't start a fuss.

(*John caresses her again. When he raises his head he notices the picture on the wall and crosses over to it with her—his arm still about her.*)

JOHN. Why, that's you and me!

EMMA. Yes, I never could part with that. You coming tomorrow morning, John, and we're gointer get married, aint we? Then we can talk over everything.

JOHN. Sure, but I aint gone yet. I don't see how come we can't make all our arrangements now.

(*Groans from bed and feeble movement.*)

Good lord, Emma, go get that doctor!

(*Emma stares at the girl and the bed and seizes a hat from a nail on the wall. She prepares to go but looks from John to bed and back again. She fumbles about the table and lowers the lamp. Goes to door and opens it. John offers the wallet. She refuses it.*)

EMMA. Doctor right around the corner. Guess I'll leave the door open so she can get some air. She won't need nothing while I'm gone, John.

(*She crosses and tucks the girl in securely and rushes out, looking backward and pushing the door wide open as she exits. John sits in the chair beside the table. Looks about him—shakes his head. The girl on the bed groans, "water," "so hot." John looks about him excitedly. Gives her a drink. Feels her forehead. Takes a clean handkerchief from his pocket and wets it and places it upon her forehead. She raises her hand to the cool object. Enter Emma running. When she sees John at the bed she is full of fury. She rushes over and jerks his shoulder around. They face each other.*)

EMMA. I knowed it! (*She strikes him.*) A half white skin. (*She rushes at him again. John staggers back and catches her hands.*)
JOHN. Emma!
EMMA (*struggles to free her hands*). Let me go so I can kill you. Come sneaking in here like a pole cat!
JOHN (*slowly, after a long pause*). So this is the woman I've been wearing over my heart like a rose for twenty years! She so despises her own skin that she can't believe any one else could love it!

(*Emma writhes to free herself.*)

JOHN. Twenty years! Twenty years of adoration, of hunger, of worship!

(On the verge of tears he crosses to door and exits quietly, closing the door after him.)

(Emma remains standing, looking dully about as if she is half asleep. There comes a knocking at the door. She rushes to open it. It is the doctor. White. She does not step aside so that he can enter.

DOCTOR. Well, shall I come in?
EMMA (*stepping aside and laughing a little*). That's right, doctor, come in.

(Doctor crosses to bed with professional air. Looks at the girl, feels the pulse and draws up the sheet over the face. He turns to her.)

DOCTOR. Why didn't you come sooner. I told you to let me know of the least change in her condition.
EMMA (*flatly*). I did come—I went for the doctor.
DOCTOR. Yes, but you waited. An hour more or less is mighty important sometimes. Why didn't you come?
EMMA (*passes hand over face*). Couldn't see.
   (Doctor looks at her curiously, then sympathetically takes out a small box of pills, and hands them to her.) Here, you're worn out. Take one of these every hour and try to get some sleep.

(He departs.)

(She puts the pill-box on the table, takes up the low rocking chair and places it by the head of the bed. She seats herself and rocks monotonously and stares out of the door. A dry sob now and then. The wind from the open door blows out the lamp and she is seen by the little light from the window rocking in an even, monotonous gait, and sobbing.)

www.ingramcontent.com/pod-product-compliance
Lightning Source LLC
Chambersburg PA
CBHW032133050726
47590CB00008B/3079